My Life's Flow

Vol.3

Taryn A Robinson

ISBN: 978-1-963919-66-0

Dedication

Dedicated to everyone that has helped me grow into the strong black woman, poet, partner, parent and person that I am today. You are the water I that I cannot live without, the current that pushes me and helps my life keep flowing.

Contents

About the Author

Taryn Robinson is an African-American poet from Sacramento, California. Her third book of poems, My Life's Flow Vol.3, is based on her experiences in her 30s and covers topics like love, politics, lost loved ones, addiction, and mental health. The poems reflect her ability to triumph over life's challenges. Readers are encouraged to push through life's struggles and find true peace, happiness, and appreciation that they are still living. Every day is another chance to smile.

23

My lioness left our pride after the seeds he gave her,
Something we couldn't deliver no matter how many shakes and shivers.

The change was abrupt, no last embrace, not knowing that was the last time we'd see her face.
Plans pushed aside, hearts torn a little,
Space, time, and misunderstanding created the largest divide.
Given the chance to mend,
Once again, have my lioness as both lover and friend.
Took me back, took me down deep, and my heart could no longer pretend.

It wasn't a fresh start, it was full of broken pieces from the start,
Shattered pieces like a broken mirror, but it was my broken heart.
We couldn't put all the pieces together because a few had already disappeared,
The most critical pieces, but I loved every single day.

My lioness is free to travel and start a new pride,
One with all the pieces, all the happiness that the new lion can provide.

My Life's Flow.

31

Heart hurts
My brain burns
My stomach is full of butterflies
The tears won't stop running down my face
Fingers twitch
The palpitations start
Warmth comes over me, but it is anger, it is frustration
Its embarrassment
It's dark, it's lonely, it's painful
All wrapped into one
I want it to end.

I don't want to feel, see nothing, hear nothing, Take 22 pills, and chill.
Drive my fist through a wall.
Take a bath and soak till my body goes numb, But I can't cause them pain, anger, frustration, embarrassment
I want it to end
My Life's Flow
Back
Back and forth and round and round,
Dizzy, confused ego bruised,
Used to hear and say "I love you," but I can't remember the sound.

Better yet, the feeling of warmth it brought me knowing I was your love,
The one, the only person you were thinking of.

But it is like we no longer fit, like OJ's glove,
Even though we once did,
Even though I considered making your next kid.

I tried and tried hard to be patient with the ups and downs,
I said to myself, maybe you just don't know how it's supposed to feel when a real one holds you down,
But we're still going round and round,
Back and forth.

I've been more patient, more loving, and more faithful than I have to any other in this world.

But that's not good enough.

All Mine

I charge my phone just to make sure that you can call

I got too used to giving the bare minimum but with you I give my all

Can't survive the hours without hearing your ringtone, yeah I'm that old

And I think about you all day, something that I constantly feel but have rarely told

For your smile i bring you tulips, you don't even care that they're the cheapest flower ever
you kiss my two lips and I give you my aloe Vera

Sprinkle me baby
Let our love seeds grow crazy

Heart of a lion, no dandy
Sweet as candy

Patience of a teacher, kindergarten
Softness and appreciation of beauty ill never trample your garden

Hold me down like we're in the notebook
You remind me of how love should be like you wrote the textbook

MY LIFE'S FLOW

So, I charge my phone just to make sure that you can call
I got too used to giving the bare minimum but with you I will always give my all

BFF

She and I go back like those things on Deville's.
I don't think ordinary people can understand how good this feels
To have someone so honest who understands your triumphs and your struggles, knows the deal,
But I have that.

Facts.

I've been a rolling stone, but that one friend is where I hang my hat.

She picks me up when I'm running on empty or when my tires go flat,
And I always run that back.

No fake and phony, never have to feel lonely, just a real one, real relationship through all our situation ships.

Been down since the 90s before selfies and shit.

She had the Nokia, and I had the Motorola.

I only had my bike to bend corners.

When she's up, I congratulate her;
When she's down, I want to pick her up.

MY LIFE'S FLOW

It'll be good if I go through life without making a new friend because she fills my cup.

The new promotion, I wish you good luck.

New car, I want to donate the bucks.

No hate, not once, not ever.

Real friends grow up, get buck, and give no fucks... together.

Bingo!

I wanted you to feel like you were winning with me.

I loved that you were a good girl who wanted to be bad for me.

The way we connected intimately was out of this world.

I felt like I won the championship the way your toes curled,
Bingo! Bingo! Bingo! As you released
And I keep going until I get it all; joy is just a piece.

I felt like I hit the jackpot.

I never had to ask if you were down because you were always about that action.

I was ready for action, but I didn't give you the correct reaction you needed to see.

I couldn't be the one you needed me to be.

We ended up being physically connected but emotionally distant, and that's all on me.

Bingo! We're too different to stay.

I'm too stubborn to say what you want me to say.

MY LIFE'S FLOW

My scars may go deeper than I thought.

I should have appreciated everything that I got.

I made you cry, and that's something I would never try.

Knowing I've become such a monster makes me want to die, but I didn't, so I'm back to my old ways.

There are many selfless, caring people these days, but my actions say I don't deserve to have one in my life.

Bingo! Nevermind. I lost.

-My Life's Flow

Chemistry

The grade is A+ for the chemistry between us, going through both the good and the bad times, and establishing trust.

There will be no stopping,
The constant heart throbbing,
Explosion of feelings,
Real shit has no ceilings.

I won't trigger you,
I'll help you.

Words penetrate my mind like she is greasing my scalp,
Testing the ambit of my devotion.

Clear Skies

It's 75 outside with clear skies,
Yet constant rain pours from my eyes.

Bloodshot,
Trying to smile like I'm happy, but I'm not.

I still feel alone even when I'm with my best friend,
Pill after pill, I try and try again.

They break the clouds, but the relief is only temporary.

The darkness I see forming from the second I wake up is oh-so-scary.

It's beautiful outside, but still I feel so ugly within.

I don't know if I'll be able ever to see the sunshine again.

My inner light and life now are dim and dead.

I'm hoping for clearer skies ahead.

Constant rain pours from my eyes,
Even though It's 75 outside with clear skies.

Coasting

In a situation so rare,
the L word is a losing game, and it's never fair.

Something lights up inside of me with just your stare.

I like things about you that I never knew I liked, starting with your hair.

The personality you have captivated me sexually,
and I'm feeling the compatibility, passionate like animals.

I want to taste every delicate inch of you like Hannibal,
Feasting on each other's souls like cannibals.

In a situation so rare,
You provide a whirlwind of emotion.

I'm not sure when it happened, but I drank your potion,
And as horrible as it sounds, I'd drink it again.
I thought I was different, thought I was better, but I stem from sin.

I want to be your friend.

I want to be your lover.

I want to lay you down like no other.

MY LIFE'S FLOW

Fire burns in my chest, down my loins, and a little deeper.

Your willingness to love is your best feature in a situation so rare.

Crime of Passion

I think I just caught a body, and nobody can stop me.

DOA at her climatic arrival, and it's a mess because I slay her DNA evidence all over the room.

They'll need CSI and SVU, changing clothes and linens, trying not to get caught up.

Things were frisky, things were risky, and I think the camera was rolling because the tripod was still up.

Mask off, so everything was exposed; it's like she's already going into rigor, the way she curled her toes.

The room smells of strawberries and champagne, yet this beautiful queen had to be slain.

The bathtub was still warm, filled with candles, bubbles, and roses. It was like a top model photo shoot; I tried so many positions and so many poses.

Leaving only one trace, it's a clear, sticky substance, no doubt water-based, with no fingerprints.

It's as if gloves were worn; indeed, this is another cold case, my third one this month.

MY LIFE'S FLOW

Should I stop? Should I continue? My third one this month, should I stop? Should I continue?...

I'm so torn.

I gotta stay away from these hoes #LifeGoals.

A Crime of Passion Perhaps,
But The Main Suspect Nobody Knows.

I Just Caught a Body.

My Life's Flow.

Crippled

She was broken, and now I am crippled.

Damaged beyond repair, tall waves of despair create so much salt in the air.

I will fix it. I will heal. I truly believe that I can get better for her and be a better woman.

I tried, and I tried to mend my broken wings.

She shut me down, face-planted in the ground.

I was so lost, but it was the wrong one I'd found.

She crippled me, leaving me shattered like glass.

Sleeping all day, drinking like a fish, making everyone else feel dismissed, and being a moody B!+@.*

Crying like a baby because it's the real her that I miss.

The pain is so paralyzing that I can no longer stand.

She crippled me the day she left me, and I never saw her again. I loved her even though I knew that she was broken.

MY LIFE'S FLOW

Now I'm torn into pieces, regretting all the words unspoken, and now I am crippled.

My Life's Flow.

Dark

Does he know what we talk about all day?
Does he know all the freaky things I make you say?
Does he know where you were the other night?
Does he appreciate that you're so tight?
Does he know I created that geyser?
Does he know I'm the only person who can take your passion to new heights?
Does he notice that you only want him with no lights?
I know you're thinking about me and how I please.

I know the thought of my work makes you weak in the knees.

Does he know you're ready to go now that you have the best?
Does he know your spot is only 3 inches deep and up to the left?
Does he pay attention and show you tricks like I show?
Does he go in as long as I go?
Do you run from him like you run from me?
Do you sometimes slip up and call him T?
Does he bend you up like a gymnast?
Does he give you sweet dreams?
Does he notice that you need scuba gear now that I get you like the ocean, at least, it seems?
If he doesn't, he will.

You know what they say, what's done in the dark...

Decisions

Decisions, decisions...
Who will win and who will lose?
What to do, what to choose?
Will this hurt? Will it bruise?
How much heartache? How much heartbreak?
Can you take it? Can I take it?
Was this true love, or was this fake?
Tears got me sinking into the drama like Ricki Lake.

Good is how I treated you,
But you feel like I cheated you.

I gave you all of me, yet I have no more to give.

Being alone, a life I don't want to live.

Decisions, decisions.

I truly dread the day you leave me.

I lose the best parts of myself on the daily.

This rollercoaster is making me sick.

We've been through the thin, but now we're stuck in the thick of it.

To keep you would kill me.

We can't go on like this anymore.

If anyone understood, I thought you'd feel me.

Decisions, decisions.

I won't be selfish.

I won't play the victim, won't play helpless; I take full responsibility.

I'm the bad guy, but you'll never be able to say I didn't try.

I kept it honest. There wasn't a reason to lie.

It's so hard to say goodbye.

I never thought the day would come when I didn't have you by my side.

Decisions, decisions...
The decision has already been made.

With every word and action, when we chose ourselves over each other, we raised our voices every time.

We lost our choice.

Deep

I want to go deep, soul deep, deeper than that spot that takes you to your peak.

If you want to make sure you need more than a nap, put yourself in a super-deep sleep.

Deep like being okay with just staring into your eyes,
Deep like telling you everything, even about those weird times with guys.

Deep like crispy-ass French fries.

I want to go deep, like fiending to hear your voice every day because you'll make everything okay.

I want to do deep, like I'm implanting myself in your uterine walls.
Pause. That got straight. Let me get back to being gay. My way.

I want to go deep, but only as deep as you'll let me.

I want to go deep, but as slowly as you need, ensure you won't regret me.

Different

I can't shake this feelin' of being a jerk, being the villain.

Not sleeping well, acting out, but you can't tell.

I'm not emotional, just overwhelmingly unlike myself—bad health, no wealth, bored and unloved like your old favorite toy left on the shelf.

Sometimes, the days fly away.

I can't tell you what I did yesterday.

Nothing memorable happened, I guess.

My mind is an overall mess.

Shopping hard, no stopping but nothing I need,
gambling hard, breaking into the bank 'til I have a panic attack and can't breathe.

Creativity is dwindling.

My imagination is getting dark, and I'm running out of words to say, the right song to play, and the light to see the potential for a new day.

I'm not giving up yet. I'm broken, but I'm worth healing.

I can shake this feeling.

My Life's Flow.

Double S

Double S like superwoman. You've always been a Superstar to me.
Natural beauty without the bundles that I wish you could see.

Double S like superwoman.

If being on nasty bitch status was your goal, you've already obtained it.

After just one night, you have me smitten and shit, emotions overflowing. I can't explain it.

Double S is like superwoman.

I've watched your lipstick poppin' 5hrs for years, and it feels like five years to me. Racing thoughts of you aren't stopping.

Double S is like a superwoman.

Being next to you warms me up, burning only with desire, begging you to feel my passion because it is wet enough to fill a cup.

Double S is like Superwoman Superfly to me.
It was indeed a pleasure to finally meet.

-My Life's Flow.

Down

I am going downtown, but the streets are clean.

Going downtown in the sheets means making a mess and leaving everything soaking wet.

I promise this trip will leave no regrets.

No violence, but the neighbors will hear your screams.

When you finish, I know you'll have the sweetest of dreams.

Sometimes, it flooded downtown, and I felt like I was going to drown.

But it's all worth it to me to hear the sounds of joy and fear, especially when you're so excited that it brings you to tears.

It's like downtown in the middle of Katrina.

Every Inch

I like to take the time to lick every inch of you and make you feel that my love is both deep and genuine.

Wearing only my birthday suit of passion,
Finally, a mental attraction.

Your rose swollen like a walnut,
I can't wait for you to crack my nut.
As it drips down your face,
I kiss you to see how I taste.
Sweet as pure cane,
This love affair is starting to drive me insane.
I like to take the time to lick every inch of you.
I need you to know how badly I desire you.
Temperatures rising, can you feel my fire as my skin burns against yours, too?
I kiss your sweat as it beads down your cheeks. Both sets.
I promise you never leave unsatisfied, upset, or with regrets.
I am sorry that I can't supply you with lovemaking.
I feel our connection get deeper when my legs are shaking and your juices sometimes flowing 2 feet away,
Leaving me with a mouthful of adoration as I think to myself, "That's bae."
That's why I'd like to take the time to lick every inch of you.

Family First

I put my family over myself, I put my family over my health.

When I wake up, my family is what I think of first.

The thought of being there for my family often keeps me sane.

I put my family first, so if I'm not happy, maybe I'm to blame.

I put my family first, and I want my mate to do the same.

I put my family first, so sometimes I can't turn up, and I'm pretty lame.

I put my family first, but I feel last.

I put my family first and undeniably have made plenty of mistakes in the past.

I've learned from my mistakes, and that's why I put family first.

I've been there and done that, and I know where true love is at.

When friends are too busy, when I feel like the hoes aren't really for me, when I fall, I'm good cause I put family first.

I've realized I have too much going on to worry about anything else. I am incredibly thirsty.

When I feel like my family doesn't put me first, I don't think I've felt anything worse.

My love is both a gift and a curse.

But still, I put my family first til I'm in a hearse.

It's ingrained in me, been this way since birth.

My family's everything to me, but how do I assess my worth?

Who will put me first?

Fiend

When it hits my veins, and my head tilts back,
No other feeling in the world can match that.

I'd kill for it, I'd steal for it,
Fetch water up a hill for it.

Just one more hit,
My eyes roll back but don't feel out of place,
My body heats up and puts a smile across my face.

I'm in the zone watching my touchdown dance,
I can't even count how many times I've lost my pants,
All for the rush like no other,
I've done a lot of bad things, starting with my mother.

But I need it, just one more hit,
Hell no, I'm not addicted, I can always quit.

Momma says she's tired of my shit,
I woke up in a car today and can't remember how I even got in it.

I am a hustler, I don't need a regular job,
I get money by any means necessary, yeah sometimes I rob.

I don't need anybody but myself,
I don't care about the government saying it's bad for my health.

Just one more hit, damn, that feels good,
Maybe when I wake up tomorrow afternoon, I might get help.

Maybe one day I'll see what it's doing to myself when getting out,
My teeth aren't even essential, my new ones even pop out.

I had to do something strange, and these came in handy,
I'm not gay, I just did what I had to do for the OG.

I needed just one more hit, which was my last.

Forgiven but not forgotten

I can forgive you and let you off the hook.

I can learn to forgive you, I even got some self-help books.

I can forgive you for all of the pain that you caused,
Tearing my heart into pieces on a rampage without pause.

Acting oblivious to my suffering mentally, physically, and emotionally,
I can forgive you because you showed me that this was NOT how love is supposed to be.

Can I forgive your selfish nature, or was it nurture?
Next time I pick a love, I won't do what you did to me. I won't hurt her.

I can forgive you for all the others that you put before me,
But if I genuinely want to be happy, I have to forgive YOU for ME.

My Life's Flow.

Gone

When the neurons that once carried excitement and hope for you no longer shoot back and forth, like World War 2,
When the butterflies no longer flutter as if jarred, left with no holes begin to lose their wings,
When you start to understand why the caged bird sings,
When the heart's rhythm becomes boring, almost monotone, and you're moving through life like a drone,
When the chemistry turns into failed experiments,
When every once in a while, you feel a small spark, a tiny reminiscence of what was once the most incredible experience,
But nothing that makes you want to stay, fly far away, before you lose yourself and the good pieces of you dwindle.

Heart Eyes

You've awakened me, heart eyes.

My heart starts to race just seeing your smiling face and having the opportunity to be in the reflection of your eyes.

You make my blood start pumping as I touch your amazingly soft thighs. Heart eyes.

You make me want to be a better person, and I know it sounds wild, but I tell no lies.

There's no sweeter sound than your orgasmic cries. Heart eyes.

I wake up with you on my mind every day. It must be because you captivate me in every way. Heart eyes.

Our vibe is so dope I can't help but smile.

I don't want to jinx it by talking about forever, but I'm happy to have you in my world, even if it's just for a little while.

I'll have heart eyes...for you.

My Life's Flow.

Home

I know that writing is supposed to be relatable, but this is not the one.

My circumstances were not debatable, so I hope no one understands where I'm coming from.

Walking down my streets captures a whirlwind of emotion. You see winos looking for the potion, everybody broke but pretending to be happy, and crackheads in pain.

All the mothers were single and just trying to maintain.

Momma made it work even when she didn't work, never hopped on a pole, never twerked.

It couldn't shelter me from the fact that there's a body on the street every week,
And all we can say is that "it must be the summer heat."

Memories fade of the OGs, like that t-shirt with his picture, so I can't remember one name.

My people catching bodies only to discover that it was a fake chain,
Doing life so his son doesn't know any better, picks up where daddy left off in hopes of helping momma get out of the stormy weather.

Instilled inner strength in me. I always wanted to dictate my destiny, not just be another victim of poverty.

I moved away almost ten years ago, but not a day goes by when it doesn't bother me.

I want the best for everyone, but some are too ignorant to realize,
Some are too afraid to open their eyes.

But I have so much more respect for a person who at least tries,
Seeing it down at the big park,
Weak ones letting bullets fly as the kids play, those clowns had no heart.

I wouldn't call it home. I just called it Oak Park.

My Life's Flow.

Honesty

Honesty comes naturally, honestly.

Suspicions outweigh the truth, and you're too blind to see.

At home but not at home,
Still not at home when I roam.

Silence of lambs and no skin-to-skin,
We used to go rounds 'til you'd tap out but now no one wins.

Matrimony 'til death do us part, but we're already apart,
Acting heartless although I have the biggest heart.

Playing the game and enjoyed a few sidelines,
But to me you're truly fine wine, your value increases over time.

Hard to explain the distance between us,
It's like Mars and Venus.

We used to be on the same page,
I guess I got less patient with age.

I guess I could've put forth more effort,
But is true love supposed to take this much work?
I know that I'm a jerk, but my honesty comes naturally, honestly.

MY LIFE'S FLOW

I've always kept it real, but your suspicions outweigh the truth and you're too blind to see.

My Life's Flow.

Honeymoon Phase

I want to make my dreams come true with you.

Share rings with you, do things that only lovers do.

Floating so high when I'm with you, cloud 9,
Always on my mind.

Throughout all of these struggles, I have faith that we'll stand the test of time.

There is no doubt that this is true.

I feel it in my heart and veins, too.

I don't care what we go through,
As long as I'm with you and you stay down for me, too.

Just as long as I can see your smile,
As long as I can stare into your eyes for a while.

We'll be in the honeymoon phase.

My Life's Flow.

I See You

I see things in you that maybe you don't see.

I see things in you, know that I wish I had in me.

I see things in you that make you sad.

I want to take it all away and be the best you've ever had.

I see some deep things in you that make me want to be wrong.

I want to show you're beautiful, no hair, no makeup, both inside and out.

I want to show you how good life can be and show you when I'm about.

I'm extra low-key, and I don't expect anything in return.

If I'm not what you need, then we will just let it burn.

I am poly for real, so I have enough room in my heart for both of your strong personalities within.

You're on that 90s shit, so what I'm saying is I want to be your homie, lover, and friend.

I will be honest, I will be dependable, and most importantly, I will be worthy.

Although I want to give you a lot, I know you're a nasty bitch and don't need anything from me.

That's a great thing because I'm a regular dude that doesn't have much money.

Although I'm usually a G with you, I want to be as sweet as honey.
I'll be your friend for as long as you let me.

With every interaction, I'll make sure you regret me.

It has been a long time, and I know a lot of things have changed, but to me, you just got more dope.

That must be why I'm hooked; I'm taking a risk, telling you soft shit, but for the best, I can only hope.

I'll keep you close and hold you tight like a teddy.

I'll be waiting patiently till you're ready.

My Life's Flow.

Inside Out

I'd like to taste from the outside in.

Drop the date and time and hold on because the ride's about to begin.

Tossing and turning like a whirlwind.

I own it, not your woman or girlfriend, and all the neighbors know it.

Most importantly, your river will show it.

Stay loyal like a wife.

Let me be the conductor of the ride of your life.

We can go rounds, but I always win, so don't fight this, and in the end, you'll lie lifeless.

Just an occasional shiver down your spine into your toes.

And that's only one of my short-term goals.

Kenya

She takes me back to my roots because she's authentic.

Skin is beautifully sun-kissed.

Style is chill, and the headwrap game is perfect.

No make-up when she wakes up.

It pulls at my heartstrings and makes me want to get my cake up.

She is the prototype, the original, and not worried about measuring to the American standards and being fake.

She is a beauty. She is poetry,
and she is art because she is authentic.

My Life's Flow.

Meditate

I think I need to meditate,
can't think straight.

Hearts racing,
Can't stop pacing.

I have no idea what I'm really facing.

I feel crazy as hell,
Rocking back and forth like I'm in a white padded cell.

I think I need to meditate,
Can't think straight.

Feelings are all over the place,
I feel pissed off and I feel sad.

I feel so confused about everything and that's making me mad.

Feel like throwing up, my stomach's fluttering like butterflies going up,
Only to be stopped by lid of the jar.

And I'm suffocating with them, it's all black right now,
I still can't see a single star.

I think I need to meditate,

I can't think straight.

My Life's Flow.

Mid Life

My crisis came early,
It may be my mid-life, but I'm only 30.

Indecisive as hell,
Acting recklessly, trying everything, not caring if I fail.

Female after female, still unbelievably unsatisfied.

Being faithful, committed, and family-oriented is out the window, but at least I tried.

Buying dumb shit,
Spending more than I have, saying, "Just charge it."

Dreaming of a better day when I wake up with hopes today will be a better day, and there's gotta be a better way.

Need more excitement,
No matter how nicely I'm treated, I can't appreciate it. I'm messing up, and I admit it.

Starting unnecessary arguments, that fuse, I lit it.

I've been running on empty lately, looking for things to get me temporarily gassed up.
Drink, hookah, and fuck, gambling like a madman pressing my luck.

I'm stuck.

My Life's Flow.

Mistake

This may be a huge mistake,
But it feels like a risk I must take.

A huge leap of faith,
I was scared out of my mind because I didn't feel safe.

Anxiety is through the roof,
It got me numbing the pain like I got a bad tooth.

It got me writing like I'm about to go into the booth,
It got me spiraling out of control because I already knew the truth.

It was good while it lasted,
But I'm having the worst time putting us in a casket.

Panic attacks are at an all-time high,
Rather than get my wings and fly,
AKA die.

MY LIFE'S FLOW

Ms. F (Teacher, Teacher)

Teacher, teach me something new.

Teacher, teacher, make my teacher fantasies come true.

You take me on a field trip and get sticky like the floors of the movie theaters used to.

Line me up to drink from your water fountain and count, 1-2-3.

Teacher, teach me something new.

Teacher, teacher, make my teacher fantasies come true.

Every time I'm in class with you, it's physical education and I love P.E.

It's more than contact sports between you and me.

All November long, I'll trace my handprints all over your body but we're not making turkeys.

You can work my body and you can work my brain,
Only teach you happiness and passion, you'll never know pain.

Teacher, teach me something new.

Teacher, teacher, make my teacher fantasies come true.

MY LIFE'S FLOW

Your body is a work of art and everything is perfect the way it's supposed to be.

Your natural beauty is the most enticing part to me.

Pardon my grammar, but I want to make you say words that you can't teach in English class.

I want to hear you yelling at the top of your lungs,
Next year you'll have to teach choir after all the high notes that you sung.

Teacher, teach me something new.

Teacher, teacher, make my teacher fantasies come true.

I've graduated.

My Life's Flow.

My Itch

One of the baddest horses in my stable,
But she wanted me to stop scratching my itch, and I couldn't.

I thought it was a match made like Hitch.

Can I get a manager to check stand 6? I need to exchange my bitch.

Their temper was so bad I sometimes worried she'd put me in a ditch.

I tried to explain that there's so much more to life than money.

I'd give up everything to spend time cuddling with my honey.

Our priorities began to differ and
Our bond began to separate, and it felt like there was nothing we could do.

With the lights off, we did not come together like gorilla glue.

Muse after muse, but we have yet to find one that we can choose from.

Ego bruised, lies told, we tried, and we tried, but that shit gets old.

I chose to leave. Not saying it was good or bad. I didn't want to wait until someone ended up dead.

MY LIFE'S FLOW

Maybe even locked up, getting shanked in the ribs,
Making lifetime bids, thinking, what about our kids?

I am calling the cops, creating TV drama.

Her family hates me, but she still checks on my mama.

She wanted me to stop scratching my itch, but I couldn't.

She was indeed one of the worst bitches in my stable.

My Life's Flow.

Mystery

My obsession with you is a mystery to me.

The hours I spend with you on my mind can fill more books than history.

How I long to spend more time consistently,
And how I want to be #1, the winner, the best you ever have in history.

No matter how different we are, there's still a powerful electricity.
Mesmerized by your sweet fruits, they're so magical that they're glittery.

You'll shine in my eyes even if you don't in your own, so don't fall for their trickery.

I see down into your soul, she's both beautiful and mysterious, don't you see?

Puzzled by wants and needs on life's confusing journey,
Guard up for protection after tragedy.

It's my pleasure to break down those walls that you thought were impenetrable.

Only by giving you the love you need, it's that simple.
Your mystery is more mystifying.

Every chance to be near you is exciting.

I'm in it for the long haul,
Your mysteriousness will never have a valedictory.

My Life's Flow.

Never

Procrastinated and now I'm castrated,
A future I never contemplated.

Never will I see your face,
Never will I hold your hand.

Never will I see you grow up to be the best man or woman.

Never will I see the first step,
Never will you take your first breath.

Never will I rub your head and sing you back to sleep.

Never will I be able to comfort you and hold you when you weep.

Procrastinated and now I'm castrated,
A future I never contemplated.

Never did I stop to realize the time wasted could've been invested in you.

Gerber grow-up plans to help have the future I never had.

Even with two moms and no dad, I'd give my all to see you smile.

Keep trying, they say, these things can take a while.

MY LIFE'S FLOW

Never will I experience the only love that's true.

Never will I have that epiphany, out of me came something as beautiful as you.

Procrastinated and now I'm castrated,
A future I never contemplated.

My Life's Flow.

Numbers

Every day I give more and more of me,
Yet you continuously feel like less of a priority.

Those numbers don't add up.

I've spent over 1000 days watching you wake up, the real you, no falsification, no makeup.

I can't count the time that you've taken up,
My thoughts, my eyes, the nights I've cried.

Spiraling down to the nights that I wish I died.

Although self-inflicted, I've never tried.

I can't count the smiles in front of the tears I hide.

My Life's Flow.

Nurse Betty

You supply everything that I need to be on cloud 9.

Morphine's flowing so I'm feeling high.

In your Winnie the Pooh scrubs, Pooh is cute but you're cuter.

Hanging onto your every word, sign, and direction like you're my math tutor.

You heal me with minimal effort.

Digging on you so deep that it hurts.

With sophistication, education, and class, there's no need to twerk.

When your shift's over, I wait all night for you to return to work.

My morning baths are everything, I'm excited like a bride to be.

On the outside, I'm silent but on the inside, I'm screaming, "Sponge me baby, sponge me."

My final days will be in bliss.

The only thing I need is your kiss, but you and I know that I'm too old to make a wish.

Where did the time go? It sure does fly.

I wasted all these years and it just passed me by.

If I had you to come home to, maybe I could live a little longer.

If I had you to live for, I could be a little bit stronger.

My Life's Flow.

Out

Today I'm breaking free of the binds that once took away my life.

My freedom, my hope, my decisions were not my own.

Throwing the shackles on the floor, massaging my wrists,
With a smile on my face waiting for the sun to shine upon me.

Free, yes I finally feel free.

What does God have in store for me?

What will I do first? I need to complete my bucket list or at least the top 5.

No money, no purse, but I have to show the world I'm worth this new life.

Where will I go? Who will I see?

Wonder if anyone missed the real me.

I'm full of hope, full of positivity.

So today I start my journey, out of bondage, my spirit feeling free and clear.

No fear, no apprehension, and no problem with tackling life on my own.
After 11 years my freedom my hope my decisions are my own
I never go back to jail again

My Life's Flow.

Papa Will

Papa, you're like a father figure to me,
Protector like I dream to be.

You didn't take shit from anybody,
Provider to so many.

Sometimes you threw a hundred like a penny,
Like a wishing well knowing you'd never get it back but only wished us well.

Gave great advice and never wanted me to fail, knowing you had my back made me want to excel.

You tried to be tough but you were always a big softie to me.

Smooth swagger from your head to your shoes.

Left with great memories of a drink in your hand, a smile on your face while listening to the blues.

Also, a man of flaws but don't we all?

Through every test, you made it through standing tall.

Beating cancer, surviving war, and just trying to maintain in these crazy times.

I know you've seen worse than I could ever put into words or rhymes.

Your mind, body, and soul hardened by your days picking cotton.

You will never be forgotten.

You were a great father to us all and sometimes spoiled us rotten.

Realizing I'll never get to see you again is a pill that's hard to swallow,
Leaving a piece of my heart forever hallowed.

Hope you know how much we love you,
Because we truly do, Papa.

My Life's Flow.

Peace

Stressing every day, I need my peace.

Not that eternal peace, just a piece.

Something nice and quiet to take me away just for a little while, maybe a day.

No traffic, just peace.

No angry customers, just peace.

No diets, no restrictions, I'll order another piece.

If I had a little piece of peace, maybe I would no longer have thoughts of being deceased.

Maybe if I had peace, I could make it another year or two.

No bad test results, just peace.

No life expectancy discussions, just peace.

Taking everything one second at a time.

Getting thoughts together and a peace of mind.
Enjoying every second and sight,

For permanent peace may come day or night.

My Life's Flow.

Perfect

Your lips are the softest I've ever felt.

Kissing you warms me up, I can't help but melt.

In May, thoughts run through my mind and of course, they're freaky.

Your body is so amazing, touching you makes my heart start racing.

Blood pressure rises, and body temperature rises.

You drive me crazy, I don't want to end up hiding in your bushes wearing disguises.

That walk is the best, standing behind you takes away all of my focus.

I want to make you happy.

I want to rub you to fall asleep without you even asking me.

I want to tell you jokes to keep you smiling.

I want to hold you down and put you in your place when you're wilding.

Give you that work to put you in the best mood.
Beat it down until you lose that attitude,

And every other time you're acting rude.

Are you so good that I own it?

Every time you say my name, you will moan it.

Kissing you warms me up, I can't help but note,
Your lips are the softest I've ever felt.

Can't wait to kiss you again.

My Life's Flow.

Quarantine Blues

Dreaming of numerous margaritas and sand between my toes.

Living my best life every day 'til I'm 90 years old.

Quarantine blues have made me re-evaluate my #lifegoals.

My Life's Flow.

Rain

Droplets from you to me.

Going deep in it, but I got good gills and good skills that allow me to breathe.

Puddles get me soaked.

I know all the spots you like poked.

No rain boots are required, I like being wet and sticky because of you.

I don't mind staying in 'til the skies return to blue.

Thunderstorms can't drown out your roars of passion.

This weather is unbelievable, we need to capture it and get the lights, camera, and action.
Our connection is electric like lightning.

Going this deep sometimes can be frightening.
It's all worth it when you tense up and get so tight that I die between your thighs.

I just might drown in your rain.

My Life's Flow.

Sabotage

Sabotage, sabotage, sabotage.

Mood swings from 0 to 100 real quick.

If you want it to be over, just quit.

Why bring me down? Why take my joy?
Why act like you truly care about my feelings and then try to play with me like a toy?

*Your mind games are f****** worthless. I see right through you.*

And you, you, you wonder why people do you the way they do.

Right now, you got me feeling like screwed you and your position.

Since you don't value your worth, let's treat you like a real nobody.

You're a verified woman but have the worst intuition.

Sabotage, sabotage, sabotage.

No one's winning, and if this was war, I'd rather be dead than be a traitor.
I only have love in my heart, that's why you'll never see me acting like a hater.

No dumbass eye rolls, accusations, and sitting with my lips stuck out.
The only thing I'll do is pout.

My love can only be tested and pushed so far.

Shit cuts me deeper than my surgical scars.

Relationships don't fail, people fail in their relationships.

After me, you'll only end up in situations.

I just wanted to live my forever, happily but you wanted to constantly.

Sabotage, sabotage, sabotage

My Life's Flow.

Side

I sit on the sidelines,
Watching time go by,
Waiting to be the only apple in your eye.

We're both eating from the same plate, but she doesn't even know you're sharing.

I'm not a monster, I'm usually nice, sweet, and caring.

You just feed me crumbs under the table.

I want to leave you alone, but I don't know if I'm truly able.

We have more drama than cable,
Because you enjoy all of the stallions in your stable.

While I'm just watching time go by,
Sitting on the sidelines.

My Life's Flow.

Ski Mask

Ski masks bust in.

My heart feels like it wants to bust out.

Guns drawn, demanding I get on my knees.

This life, I'm not about.

Start off tough, fight, yell, scream, and shout.

Then I cry, I beg, "Please,
Just take me. I'll give you everything I have, leave them alone."

In this moment, I gladly sacrifice myself so my kids can have the opportunity to do the same for their own.

I really wish I would've been home alone.

Click-clack, so it's now fully loaded. Now the tears begin to flash flood.

That's when I hear, "Shut the hell up, blood."

My jaw hurts after that .45 across my face.

Hope my life doesn't become a feature on Cold Case.
Dripping, vision blurry, but I'm not trippin'.

MY LIFE'S FLOW

My family's safe, so I've already accomplished my mission.

I close my eyes and get ready for the end.

"Lord, please forgive me for my sins."

A loud bang goes off, then complete silence.

I lost my life due to another case of senseless violence

My Life's Flow.

Snapped

I think I really got away with it this time.

Interchanging shots of Patron and margaritas, partying like everything is fine.

Mentally going down the checklist.

Checked for skin under the nails, all 10 clipped.

Took the glasses of wine that we sipped, Arbor Mist.

Left the body cleaner than I found her, I gently wiped away all her sins with bleach.

There's so much blood that I wish I was a leech.

Cleaned the place like I was trying to get rid of the coronavirus.

My adrenaline was so turned up as I watched the life drain from her iris.

Created organized chaos; now nothing makes sense, even Dexter can't analyze the blood sprays.

Looks like I danced in it like a 6-year-old in a puddle on one of Seattle's rainiest days.

MY LIFE'S FLOW

No witness, check, cell phone destroyed but the SIM taken.

Muffled all the sounds, no arguments preceded my episode, I just snapped.

She cheated on me; this wasn't my fault. I truly loved her, no cap.

The thought of him with her was apparently too much to bear.

Next thing I knew, I was dragging her body downstairs.

Knuckles swollen and bloody.

My once beautiful queen is now so disfigured and ugly,
Wearing the HDMI cord like a necklace.

Never even knew that I was capable of this.

I think I got away with it this time.

Interchanging shots of Patron and margaritas, partying like everything is fine.

But it's her I miss when I was hers and she was mine.

My Life's Flow.

So Good

You stay on my mind all day,
You make my heart beat and our bodies warm with passion, always.

I want to tell you about my good days and hold you all night through all of your bad days.

I drip at the sight of you,
Running through my brain all day, there's no hiding you.

Make me want to do some real gay shit like riding you.

You make me feel like building trust and confiding in you.
My feelings keep popping out, there's no hiding them from you.

Scared AF of the day you say, "Let's just be friends," because we're amazing lovers.
I smile uncontrollably, both in and on top of the covers.

Talking to you for hours is just fine with me.

I love watching you while you tell me all your crazy stories.

I want to be the one to take away your worries.
You make me feel so good... like T-Pain said.

My Life's Flow.

Stimulus

I call you my stimulus because you made me happy,
Had me feeling like a boss but only for a few weeks.

Then I was back to being broke, back to being a struggling artist, back to being lonely AF and missing my cheeks.

Temporary love as usual.

Temporary wealth, we've all seen those tax time visuals.

I was rich in love, rich in pleasure, rich in you.

What's left now, I have nothing and no clue.

I just know that you're gone, just like my stimulus.

My Life's Flow.

Team No Sleep

Wish I worried about something real.

Wish darkness wasn't the only emotion I'm able to feel.

Wish my smile wasn't so fake.

Wish I didn't understand the women who drive to Lake and never hit the brake.

Missing sleep, that good sleep, so deep, restful, restoring the old me.

Not the fragile pieces that have all been assembled with Dollar Tree glue.

I'm just waiting for someone to ask, "How are you?"

And wait for the reply.

Although 9 times out of 10 my answer will be a lie.

A teeny tiny lie to shield others from the pain, stress, and worry about me.
I'm just a damaged, disposable, dark disaster, but sometimes I miss the real T.
The T that was happy, the T with the best jokes, T who had a natural glow, giggled from a natural high.

MY LIFE'S FLOW

Not the new me that feels low and feels numb and just lets the days fly by.

Hoping to get to my lucky day where I get my energy back.

Everything feels good and right in the world and I make plans to get my life back on track.

Then without warning it's gone, all hope, energy, and my light, gone. Can't sleep, toss and turn until dawn.

But that's all I do... stay up.

*In a constant battle between worrying over everything and not giving a single F@*k.*

Wish I worried about something real.

Wish darkness wasn't the only emotion I'm able to feel.

My Life's Flow.

That Good

I miss that good
That special delivery that only you could
That earth shattering
Neighbor maddening
That good

Body parts rushing with blood hard as wood
Never stop think about whether or not we should
Going on and on like the little engine that could
That good

That slip and slide
Up and down Rollercoaster ride
Creating ocean waves until we lose the tide
Clothes on or off or just pulled to the side
That good

That intense feeling eyes rolling back screaming as if to create holes in the ceiling
No control over anything just smiling and leaking
That happiest times in the world are when our peak is reaching
Neutrons firing like fireworks
Getting winded, taking a break and then doing it again
And again cuz you got that good.

My Life's Flow.

Thinking

Thinking of you and all if things i wish we could do
Places we could see
Places to be free and act out the chemistry passionately
Lips would touch, hearts would race

Me knowing i finally have the green light because of the look on your face
Your body I would taste
And whenever you needed more i say "anytime any place."
Taking you to new heights

Have you on cloud nine just enjoying the sights
No fuss no fights
But we could get rough if you'd like
Tiny scratch tender bites and the excitement of you being mine for the night makes everything feel so right
My embrace is the tightest of tight

Dont want to let you out of my sight
Die in yours arms i just might
Look at the passion and sparks that you ignite
Like fireworks on the 4th night of july

I wanna use all my frequent flyer miles cause you're so fly
All truth no lies
Crossing lines cause when im with you its hard to stay in my lane
As time goes by my passion,curiousity and lust just turn into pain

I had to kick that realness with everything to lose and nothing to gain
And nothing was the same

My Life's Flow.

TIKO

My Tiko....smart, funny and nasty...almost as cool as me
Tiko..... caring and crazy but committed to me and only me her T and proud to be

Tiko..... my baby, my friend and my equal
Tiko...so good makes me think there may not be a sequel
Tiko...with a smile so cute yet mischievous
Tiko.....the way you give me that look...I know it's time to disrobe get freaky and devious

Tiko...makes me wanna do better
Tiko...makes me less afraid of the word "together"
Tiko...i think you may be strong enough to get through my flaws, poly ways and our stormy weather

Tiko.....my tiko...in such a short time I cannot begin to lost the things you've taught me
Tiko...you're different, you intrigue me and you got me My Tiko

My Life's Flow

Time Will Tell

There was a time
A time of happiness
A time with no cattiness
A time of pure love

A time where you were all that I could think of
A time of passion
A time of undeniable attraction
A time of you and me becoming us

A time when seeing you every second was a must
There was a time
That time is no more
The time is now painful

The Time no longer allows me to be faithful
The time where we're ungrateful
A time where moves seem calculated to be hateful

My Life's Flow.

Time

I Wonder if we can fix it
Time heals all wounds but I wonder if time can fix this
Trust issues came in stealth
Stole our mental health

We've become so easily Irritated to the max
Even in situations that once were nothing and conversations were more lax
Now erupt like an angry volcano destroying the world we built together

Melting down our hopes, bonds and love that we thought would last forever Everything is burned down to the ground now and I honestly don't know if we can rebuild

Or are we scarred too deep
Tossing and turning when I'm sober losing sleep
This was my last love and one that I thought I could keep
Perhaps I don't deserve it or perhaps I'm just too weak

But I do wonder if we can fix it
If Time heals all wounds, I wonder if time can fix this
But I guess only God will be the judge and the witness

My Life's Flow

Trial and Error

Try so hard to be the best person i can be
But you don't see me
I try to show love and compassion as of they were my own but you dont see me

I try to be reasonable make my emotions less seasonal but you dont see me

I try to love you through the changes mind body and financial but you dont see me

I try to dig deep find the root or our stress and confusion but you dont see me

I try to be patient take a step back even when i feel like causing bruises and contusions but you dont see me

My true self is never free when you're around i feel buried so deep underground but you dont see me

Trying to let my light shine but like a firefly in a jar my light can only glow so far but you dont see me you really dont see me

To the point where even i can no longer see me

My hopes, dreams and happiness dwindle before me
I continuously try but Your reactions to my efforts....floor me

MY LIFE'S FLOW

I try,i try but this mary-go-round bores me
I wish i could feel like you adore me but you dont even see me

So it's best that we no longer see eachother
Trial and error

My Life's Flow.

VOL.3

Thank you for supporting my little book of rhymes
Something that has helped navigate through both good and bad times

The writing thats helped me find....this little light of mine
Even when faced with the pain & darkness caused by my own mind
The pen and paper that make me stop and think before taking a leap numerous times

The creative juices that have convinced my muses to even give me a moment of their time

Shaped my relationships into the stellar loves without a dime
Even poetically penned my love of suspense, horror and crime
My pen again has saved my life both mentally, physically and emotionally

My pen is the best thing for me, always there & always kind
Thank you for supporting my little book of rhymes

My Life's Flow.

Water

Water can be smooth

Water can take you to your tomb

Water Can be rough

Water goes deep, swimming miles and miles makes you tough

Water can even kill you Water powers our internal machines

A beauty beach in the water front appears in most out dreams

Water can be the most beautiful sight you will ever see or the last

Water seems like it has a mind of its own down you dare anger it
Water thought to be posiddeons kingdom

My Life's Flow.

Wish

I wish that I could be as cold as ice

I wish i could destroy your smiles without even thinking twice

I wish you could see the inside of my soul

I Wish that yours wasn't buried in coals

I wish my happiness was just one of your goals

I wish you wanted this like I do

I wish whenever you whispered the words...that love was actually true

I wish you stopped making my eyes drown in tears

I wish you would let go of those suspicions, insecurities and fears

I wish I was important enough for you to want to keep me

I wish it wasn't so easy for you to get up and leave me

I wish that making this Birthday Wish actually made it come true
Maybe then I'd still have you

My Life's Flow.

Wonder Woman

I wonder if we stopped conquering mountains and chasing waterfalls
could our relationship stand tall like we're built "Ford Tough"

I wonder if I had my eyes removed if you'd still worry about being pretty enough

I wonder if I only had a landline no more swipe to unlock if you would believe that you have the key to my heart

I wonder if I deactivated all accounts if we would have a fresh start
I wonder if we would have things to talk about

I wonder if a permanent smile would take the place of your current permanent pout

I wonder if it would still be so easy for you to turn your back while I am talking or just walk out

I wonder if we would still be able to connect one on one or if we'd be in a drought

I wonder if we no longer search for new lands and taste new spice and see new peaks, As through Ds

I wonder if we no longer dive into different oceans and smack glass bottoms of those seas

I wonder if things would be okay when its just you and me

I wonder if we stopped slaying the beautiful ones from state to state
Would we still have a pleasant fate

My Life's Flow.

Worry

I worry too

I worry about losing you

I worry about deep down internally bruising you

I worry about losing this one love that is undeniably true

I worry too I worry about not seeing you I worry about not being with you

I worry that one day I won't be breathing with you

I worry about the truth being no other makes me feel quite like you do

I worry about stretching my legs all the way across the bed and not bumping into you

I worry too

I worry about getting old alone

I worry there will be no one to inspire my poems

I worry and keep it hidden deep down like the catacombs

I worry with a smile on my face I worry everytime that we hug this could be our last embrace

I worry too I worry myself til i turn green but there's no mountain dew
Sick to my stomach with the though of losing you

I worry too

My Life's Flow

“Thank you for reading.”

www.ingramcontent.com/pod-product-compliance
Lightning Source LLC
LaVergne TN
LVHW011031110826
845149LV00015B/3370